JESSIE &

Heaven ON EARTH Marriage

30 DAYS OF EMPOWERMENT

Heaven On Earth Marriage "*30 Days of Empowerment*"

Publisher: J&K Publishing
Cover Design by: Tamika Hall
Photography by: Christopher Rojas
ISBN-13: 978-1540555885

Printed in the United States of America

For Media Reviews and to order additional copies please contact:

Email: heavenonearthmarriage@gmail.com
Website:
www.heavenonearthmarriageministry.com
www.kendrayadams.com

Acknowledgements

We honor God and are grateful to all who have poured into our lives and given us wisdom in the area of marriage.

To our beloved parents, Jesse C. Adams, Sr., Janie Adams, James Ellis, Sr. and Valarie Ellis. Had it not been for you, we wouldn't be here. Giving birth to us was all a part of God's plan to bring us to where we are today, serving to empower couples to have a successful marriage.

To our children, Jesse (Terra), Jessica (Julius) and our grandchildren. We are so blessed to be your parents. Thank you for your love and continuous support.

Dr. Rickie L. White and Dr. Debra White, for being marriage mentors and sharing invaluable knowledge and wisdom on how to make marriage work. Thirty one years ago, you took countless hours to counsel with us as we prepared for marriage. For many years after that, you continued to give us guidance. We can still hear your voice instilling wisdom to last a lifetime. We remain forever grateful for your outpour of love and embracing us at a critical time in our lives.

Dr. Charles E. Perry, Jr. and Lady Charlette Perry, for your pastoral leadership and love. You have been faithful and consistent examples of what a Kingdom marriage should look like. You've challenged us and opened our eyes to see covenant in a new light which has been a tremendous blessing to our marriage. It's an honor to serve with our family at Word of Restoration International Church where marriages are being restored by the word of God.

To all of our extended family. We love you all. Thank you for your love and support throughout the years.

To our inner circle of friends/accountability partners. We are so grateful for the joyous marriage memories you have been a part of creating. We are in it to win it!

To all of the couples we have mentored throughout the years. God is Faithful! We are grateful for our divine connection.

To our fellow co-harts who are on the front line waging war against divorce. May God continue to bless the work of your hands. Your labor is not in vain.

Finally, thank you to every man and woman across the globe who continue to set the standard for a Godly marriage showing the world that marriage still works!

Dedication

Who Would Have Imagined?

By: Kendra Adams

Who would have imagined
we would be here today?
The odds all against us,
it seemed as if there was no way.

I was a teenage girl, when I was
Rescued By Love,
You were an answered prayer
from heaven above.

We took in knowledge and wisdom with a
willingness to learn and see,
all that God created a covenant marriage to be.

We've overcome challenges,
some barely survived,
But now we are celebrating ...
Baby, our marriage is ***ALIVE!***

We are standing firm upon the foundation of
God's word, in a world where strong marriages
seem really absurd.

To be a visible demonstration of God's
power and love,
a reality that we love to speak of.

Who would have imagined when
our parents gave birth,
that they were creating a love that would be
Heaven on Earth.

To have and to hold until death do us part,
inscribing our love, deep into God's heart

Sharing the message, that marriage does work ....
Be Encouraged, ***Stay Strong*** and
Put the Principles to Work!

God made a Queen for You, and a King for Me
Jessie, our love will last throughout eternity.

I Love You

Table of Contents

Introduction

On May 4, 2016, Jessie and I celebrated thirty-one years of marriage. We are grateful to God for all that He has done through our marriage and in the lives of couples everywhere who are staying the journey and winning in their covenant relationship. In this day and time, longevity in marriage definitely deserves to be celebrated. To commemorate the entrance into our third decade of marriage, we've created this book to share, "***30 Days of Empowerment,***" with couples.

The Bible reads, "*I came that they may have life, and have it abundantly.*" (See John 10:10) This promise includes every area of our life, including our marriage. It was never God's intent for couples to live a life of struggle and toleration. This doesn't mean that you won't have challenges, but you learn to navigate through every season of marriage with faith and expectancy for *better* in your marriage relationship.

This book is derived from biblical truths and practical principles that have helped to encourage, strengthen and empower us in our marriage journey. We believe that marriage should be lived out purposefully and joyfully so that we may be a reflection of God's love in the earth and a visible demonstration of Christ's relationship to the Church. By doing this, we set ourselves up to flourish and experience ***Heaven on Earth*** in our marriage relationship.

Ecclesiastes 4:12 (KJV) says, *"And if one prevail against him, two shall withstand him; and a threefold cord is not quickly broken."* Our foundation, our strength and our will to endure stems from our love for Christ and our desire to please Him first. By loving Christ, we've learned how to love each other. He is the pillar of our marriage. He is the glue that holds us together. He is the foundation on which we stand. We acknowledge and recognize that we would not have a fruitful marriage nor be where we are today without God.

Our prayer is that these ***"30 Days of Empowerment"*** will be a blessing to you and your spouse. As you read this book, may the presence of God empower you, encourage you and speak to you concerning your marriage. ***We believe this book will unveil wisdom and spiritual guidance based on the word of God, to not only fuel your faith to fight for your marriage, but also enhance the quality of your marriage relationship.*** We speak blessings over your marriage. May you be strengthened, refreshed and may your love continue to flourish so that you may always experience God's best in your covenant as husband and wife.

God has equipped and empowered us all to have great marriages, but we must choose to work the principles that correct, restore, strengthen and build our marriage relationship. It takes work and it takes patience, but stay committed to cultivating your marriage so that you may experience the beauty and harvest of your covenant as husband and wife.

Abundant Blessings,

Jessie & Kendra

Day 1

A New Beginning

Throughout the year, there are moments when we all reflect on our accomplishments and begin to focus on goals for the coming year. These goals may consist of getting closer to God, losing weight, looking for new careers or even strengthening our financial portfolio. Just as we evaluate all of these areas in our life, we should also look at the state of our marriage to see what areas need to be changed, improved, corrected or downright overhauled. We should keep in mind that even if we have blown it before, it's never too late for a new beginning.

As believers, we are ambassadors (authorized representatives) for Christ. 2 Corinthians 5:20 (AMP) reads, "So we are ambassadors for Christ, as though God were making His appeal through us; we [as Christ's representatives] plead with you on behalf of Christ to be reconciled to God."

As Christ representatives, we are not only commissioned to share the good news of Jesus Christ, but we should effectively represent God in every area of our life, including our marriage. Ask yourself this question, "*Does my marriage reflect a Kingdom marriage? What does God see when He looks at our marriage relationship?*

We should never get so comfortable in our role as husband or wife that we forget that we are Christ's representatives - even in our marriage. Many times when challenges arise, we want God to shine the light on our spouse, when in actuality there are adjustments that we need to make in our own lives. Sometimes we need to forgive, adjust our attitude or simply do something "*extra*" to show love towards our spouse. The good news is, even if we've fallen short in some areas, it's never too late for a new beginning.

To create a new beginning in your marriage may mean getting back to the basics - that is, strengthening the foundation of your marriage. If the foundation of a building has cracks, eventually it's going to give and everything attached will be weakened and eventually collapse. Securing a solid foundation in marriage is vital. ***What is your marriage standing on? If your marriage is to stand the test of time and weather the storm, it must be built on a solid foundation - that foundation is Jesus Christ.***

Many who are searching for a better marriage may need to first begin a personal journey of transformation by accepting Jesus Christ as his/her Lord and Savior. Romans 10:9-

10 says, "That if thou shalt confess why thy mouth the Lord Jesus, and shalt believe in thine heart that God hath raised him from the dead, thou shalt be saved. For with the heart man believeth unto righteousness; and with the mouth confession is made unto salvation."

Once we accept Jesus Christ as Lord and Savior, we receive a new beginning. 2 Corinthians 5:17 reads, "Therefore, if any man be in Christ, he is a new creature: old things are passed away; behold all things become new. Praise the Lord!

With this new beginning, we should seek God through prayer and study of the bible so that we can learn how to live a Christ-like lifestyle, and our relationship with God can continue to grow.

This new beginning will not only cause growth and change in your personal life, but will ultimately be reflected in your relationship with your spouse.

Prayer:

Father, thank You for making all things new. Your word declares that if I confess with my mouth the Lord Jesus and believe in my heart that you raised Him from the dead, I shall be saved. Lord, I ask that you come into my life. Create in me a clean heart and renew a right spirit within me. I repent of my sins and ask for your forgiveness. I receive you as my Lord and Savior. Thank you for saving me. Thank you for my new beginning. Thank you that our marriage is built upon a solid foundation and You will get glory through this union.

In Jesus' Name, Amen.

Day 2

A Marriage That Reflects Christ

Have you ever asked the question, *"Lord, why am I married to this person*?" I think it's safe to say that many couples have thought about this question at one time or another. Perhaps it was during the aftermath of an argument or out of pure curiosity. It wasn't until several years into our marriage, that I asked God this question with the serious intent of wanting to know the greater purpose of why the two of us became one. As I meditated on this question, I was led to the following three passages of scripture:

In Genesis 1:27-28 we read (KJV) "So God created man in his own image, in the image of God created he him; male and female created he them. And God blessed them, and God said unto them, "Be fruitful and multiply, and replenish the earth, and subdue it; and have dominion over the fish of the sea, and over the fowl of the air, and over every living thing that moveth upon the earth."

In Genesis 2:22-24, we read (KJV) "And the rib, which the LORD God had taken from man, made he a woman, and brought her unto the man. And Adam said, This is now bone of my bones, and flesh of my flesh: she shall be called Woman, because she was taken out of Man. Therefore shall a man leave his father and his mother, and shall cleave unto his wife: and they shall be one flesh."

Then, in Ephesians 5:22-32, we read where the Apostle Paul shares a comparison of Christ's relationship with the body of Christ as a model for marriage. This analogy displays a vivid picture of what the covenant of marriage should look like, the guiding principles and order that will lead you into a successful marriage relationship.

In following the scripture blueprint, it's safe to say that God created man and woman to be a reflection of Him (*His character and glory*). As we enter into covenant and become united as one, the union of marriage is to then demonstrate to the world what Christ's love for the church looks like. ***Wow! Think about that for a moment!*** **Our marriage should "*look like*" Christ to others who see it**. They should see the characteristics of Christ shining through our relationship. Finally, as husband and wife, we should be careful to protect the covenant and exercise the authority that God has given to us to keep the devil out of our marriage!

Prayer:

Father, thank You for the covenant of marriage and thank You for my spouse. Let our marriage be a reflection of Christ's love in the earth. Expose and remove any dark area in our lives. Let the light of Your word shine forth and may the fruit of the Spirit (love, joy, peace, longsuffering, gentleness, goodness and faith) dominate in our actions toward You and each other.

In Jesus' Name, Amen.

Day 3

Bringing a Valuable Presence to Your Marriage

In marriage, we are continually evolving. As we grow in our relationship, we should pay close attention to the distinct characteristics that our spouse possesses. The Bible says we are fearfully and wonderfully made (see Psalm 139:14). God knew exactly what He was doing when He created your spouse.

Here are a few questions for you to think about. *What does your spouse like? What does your spouse dislike? What are your spouse's preferences? What natural and spiritual gifts do your spouse possess?* These unique traits should be identified. Over a period of time, you will eventually discover how your differences can actually be a benefit and not a barrier to your marriage. In other words, you will see how you both complement each other and bring a valuable presence to the marriage.

For example, I know that I am a "people person." I enjoy socializing, venturing out and meeting new people. Jessie is an observer and less social. He's usually quiet until he gets to know a person. We complement one another because I encourage Jessie to explore and try new and different things. This helps him to enjoy life and see bigger than where we are. On the other hand, Jessie is a "seer" and notices a lot about people that I've sometimes casually missed. He's given me insight regarding situations that have become clear to me over a period of time. We recognize that both of us bring a valuable presence to our marriage, and we've seen over and over again how our differences have helped to navigate us through life's experiences involving our household, extended family, ministry and careers.

God has a purpose and a plan for your marriage that is far greater than thousands of dollars spent on a wedding, houses or other material possessions. Your marriage is unique and your marriage has a purpose. Together, the both of you are a powerful force when you recognize the gifts that each of you possess and utilize them to bring flavor and not friction to your marriage relationship.

Think about how you and your spouse complement each other. Can you see how you both bring a valuable presence to your marriage relationship? Take a moment to write down your spouse's unique characteristics and share with him or her how they bring a valuable presence to your marriage.

Prayer:

Thank You Lord that we are fearfully and wonderfully made. Help us to appreciate the gift we have in our spouse and not allow our differences to divide us. We embrace each other's uniqueness, and build up each other in areas of weakness. We declare that our best days are NOW as we commit to walk in the spirit of unity and oneness. In Jesus' Name, Amen.

Day 4

Stay In Your Lane

One evening, Jessie and I watched a funny episode of the sitcom, "The Kings of Queens." Although comical, this particular episode contained a great message. Doug and Carrie are the main characters. Doug is a delivery man and Carrie is a secretary. In this episode, they are trying to live out the life of another couple they envy. Everything the one couple did, Doug and Carrie tried to emulate it – at all costs. As we watched this humorous episode, I thought about the uniqueness of each marriage and how it is important that we not allow ourselves to get caught up in trying to be like another couple, especially when we don't know the cost that the other couple had to pay to get to where they are today.

In marriage, we must learn to *"stay in our lane,"* and keep our eyes on the road that God has prepared just for us. There will always be detours and distractions that will attempt to get us off of our assigned path. Each time that we consider jumping into another couple's lane, we forego a greater opportunity to serve others by sharing the uniqueness God has placed within our marriage.

Let me make it personal. If Jessie and I become so consumed with trying to walk in the shoes of another couple by trying to be like them and emulate everything they do, we will never tap into the unique purpose that God has for *our* marriage. This doesn't mean that we can't have similar goals. The danger is when we become so much more focused on what other people are *doing* – and what they *have*, that we can't focus on our own personal journey and be grateful for what we have, where we are going and how we both can be a blessing to others along the way.

You see, despite how you came together, once you said, *"I Do,"* you made entrance into a lifelong covenant and a new life of *togetherness* was born. In this new life as husband and wife, we must remember that we are not married just to be married. God has a greater plan that many couples never discover because when challenges come, they *"flee"* instead of *"fight."* They allow rocks and boulders in the road to get them off of their path. They give attention to distractions that move them off of their designated lane and cause them to abandon the purpose God intended for their marriage.

Some couples are together for ministry, some to birth leaders, some to partner in business, some to mentor other couples, some to simply be a blessing to others. Whatever the case may be, remember to *stay in your lane*, be thankful for where you are, beware of distractions, stay committed to the covenant and enjoy the journey. At the designated time, you will reach your destination and God will reveal Himself to you both in a glorious way!

Prayer:

Father, thank you that we won't be anxious for anything and we won't abandon the process of growth and maturity in our marriage. Help us to stay in our lane and remain focused on Your will for our lives. We know that the manifestation of those things we envision for our marriage is yet for an appointed time and we thank You that in that perfect timing, all things will be abundantly supplied. We embrace our journey together and thank You in advance for guiding us to a rich and fruitful destination.

In the name of Jesus', Amen.

Day 5

"Trusting God for Your Marriage"

What does it mean to say, I'm trusting God for my marriage? Many of us easily make this statement, but are we really trusting God concerning our marriage?

Think about this...*How many times have you tried to fix the broken pieces in your relationship? How many times have you tried to take things into your own hands? How many times have you tried to change your spouse? Did your plan work?* The Bible says, "Blessed is the man that trusteth in the Lord, and whose hope the Lord is." (See Jeremiah 17:7)

To trust God means to put our *total* confidence in Him. It is an attitude of the heart that sees beyond the circumstance at hand. Trusting God for our marriage takes more than saying what we are "*going to do*," but we must act on it. We must make a decision to trust God, even when we feel that we can't trust our spouse. *Did you get that*?

The Bible says, "Trust in the Lord with all thine heart; and lean not unto thine own understanding. In all thine ways acknowledge Him, and He shall direct thy paths." (See Proverbs 3:5-6).

Husband and wives must get back to trusting God for whatever issues arise in their marriage. Many marriages fail because couples are getting fed lies from outside influences. They govern their marriage by the world's standard and reject God's word as it relates to their marriage. They say what they see, instead of declaring the truth of God's word. They give up on trusting God and as a result, they fail to see recovery in their marriage relationship.

I love the movie "War Room" because it gives a powerful demonstration of what happens when prayer is established in a home. A marriage went from turmoil to triumph as a wife begins to fight for her family, despite how contrary her husband is acting. One of the main characters, Miss Ciara says, "*Victories don't come by accident*!" This is a reminder that we must be intentional in prayer and consistent with our confessions. We must fill our mind with the word of God and *agree* with God concerning our marriage.

Once we put the word on our situation and give it to God, our position is to listen, obey and trust God for the results. After all, God created marriage so why not go back to the source?

Prayer:

Father, thank you for a renewed strength as I stand strong and trust You concerning my marriage. No matter how things appear in the natural realm, I choose to believe Your word concerning my marriage. I walk by faith and not by sight. I decree and declare that all things are coming into order in my home and my marriage is aligned with Your perfect will.

In Jesus' Name, Amen.

Day 6

Put the S.P.A.R.K. Back Into Your Marriage!

Has your marriage fallen into a rut? If so, it's time to put the S.P.A.R.K. back into your marriage!

Many of us are living in a fast-paced environment. We are constantly moving. We have families, businesses, school, extra-curricular activities, volunteer work and ministry commitments. It's easy to find yourself too busy to have times of intimacy with your spouse. If the routine continues, you'll begin to feel as if your marriage is dead, boring, dry...**JUST TIRED**!! Well, guess what? You don't have to let your marriage stay in a rut. Make a decision to ***PUT THE S.P.A.R.K. BACK INTO YOUR MARRIAGE*****!**

Having a great marriage doesn't come without challenges. However, times of intimacy, romance and plain ole' fun can outweigh the difficult times. Over the years, we've grown to understand the importance of making our marriage a priority. We've learned that we can't continuously pour into the lives of all those around us and neglect each other.

Can I be real with you? In marriage, you don't always feel up to spontaneous or romantic activity, but you put forth the extra effort because you realize how important and special intimate times are in a marriage relationship. These are priceless moments that create a connection. Jessie and I have embraced these five principles in our marriage to keep the ***S.P.A.R.K*** alive. We've seen the fruit of acting on these principles and believe that your marriage can be blessed by them also, if applied.

S - ***Settle Unresolved Issues***: Why? Quite simple. If issues are not resolved, more than likely there will be tension in the household. Do what is necessary to alleviate division in your home. Forgive, communicate or even seek outside counsel if necessary. Don't allow conflict to dominate the environment in your home.

P - ***Purpose To Do Something Different***: Break the routine. You remember how you use to be spontaneous? Instead of complaining that your marriage is boring, take initiative to do something different. ***Lighten up! Stop being so serious and have fun!*** Adjust your calendar to spend time with your spouse. Plan a movie night, go to the park, have a picnic, hug, kiss and flirt like you used too. Whatever the effort, ***make it your best***!

A - ***Appreciate and Affirm One Another***: Do little things to show your spouse how much you appreciate him/her. Tell your spouse, "*I love you.*" Surprise your spouse with a, "*just because*" gift. Leave a random, "*Thank You*" note. Encourage and compliment your spouse. Cuddle and tell your spouse how much he or she means to you.

R - ***Rekindle the Romance***: When it seems the romance has died, just fire it back up! Don't wait for your spouse to initiate – *Just do it*! Some fun ideas you may want to consider are:

- send flowers
- mail a love letter to your spouse's job
- give romantic coupons to redeem
- get cozy on the sofa
- send a flirtatious text
- hold hands, embrace, give gentle kisses
- take showers together
- take a walk together
- break out with a spontaneous dance to your favorite love song
- wear sexy lingerie
- dim the lights, burn candles and create magical moments

Tap into your creativity to make intimate times memorable!

K- *Keep Yourself Up*: Who doesn't want an attractive spouse? Let's do what is necessary to keep ourselves up. Never take your spouse for granted by letting yourself go. Exercise and make adjustments to embrace a healthy lifestyle. Make sure personal hygiene, undergarments, hair, clothing, etc. are at your personal best. Of course we all know that we can't be "camera-ready" 24-7, but every now and then we should make an extra effort to spruce up and give our spouse something good to behold!

Prayer:

Father, open our eyes to see areas that lack nurturing in our marriage relationship. We speak life to every dead area in our marriage. Give us creative ideas to connect and romantic ways to reach each other. Rekindle the passion and put the S.P.A.RK back into our marriage. Let us never take each other for granted.

In Jesus' Name, Amen.

Day 7

Safeguard Your Marriage

In marriage, it is important to be wise, observant, as well as proactive in safeguarding your marriage relationship. The Bible says, *"Get wisdom – it's worth more than money; choose insight over income every time. The road of right living bypasses evil; watch your step and save your life."* (See Proverbs 16:16-17 MSG)

Many couples have been blind-sided by situations that could have easily been avoided had they made an effort to safeguard their marriage. To safeguard something means to put measures in place to serve as a protection or defense.

Here are five ways that you can safeguard your marriage:

1) **Keep your personal relationship with God in check**: As we spend time with God and study the word of God, our relationship with Him is strengthened. We begin to understand His nature and embrace Godly principles that govern our life and marriage. By doing this, it helps us to stay focused on pleasing God and doing

what is necessary to uphold the covenant, even when expectations in the marriage aren't met.

2) **Communicate:** It's the little issues that are not addressed that can eventually turn into major obstacles. It is very important to keep an open dialogue in a marriage relationship. A quote from Norm Wright says, "*Communication is to Love what Blood is to Life.*" When communicating with your spouse remember the following. It will go a long way:
    - Be respectful (it's not always what you say, but how you say it)
    - Be "present" and give your undivided attention (remove distractions; i.e. phone, TV, etc.)
    - Be sensitive (if it's important to your spouse, it should be important to you)
    - Be attentive to what is *not* being said (some spouses have difficulty expressing themselves); be observant of your spouse's body language
    - Be careful to **think** before you respond (words can't be taken back)

- Be honest, but speak the truth in love (see Ephesians 4:15)
- Be a reflective listener (listen carefully and repeat what your spouse said to make sure you fully understand the concern)
- Be ready to work out a solution

3) **Set Boundaries:** In marriage, you should be careful to set boundaries with outside acquaintances. In this day and time, married men and women are comfortable with friends of the opposite sex. Sometimes friendships can grow beyond healthy boundaries with another man (for the wife) or woman (for the husband). This has become especially common in the workplace and unfortunately in the body of Christ. If you find yourself looking forward to sharing intimate conversations with another person of the opposite sex other than your spouse, that's a signal that you've become laxed in observing boundaries in the relationship. Our spouse should be our confidant. Never put another man or woman before your spouse. Setting boundaries will also help to protect trust in the marriage.

4) **Accountability:** Our first and foremost accountability should be to God. However, God uses people in our lives to help us remain accountable in affairs concerning our lives. Who do you have in your inner circle? Do they help or hinder your marriage? Are they speaking positive or negative into your marriage? Proverbs 27:17 (NIV) says, *as iron sharpens iron, so one person sharpens another.* We believe that every couple should have a marriage mentor. This is someone that you and your spouse can trust and communicate with. They should have a measure of success in their marriage and be able to pour into your marriage Godly counsel, encouragement, advice and correction, if needed.

5) **Quality Time:** Nothing says, "I love you," like full, undivided attention. This strengthens your marriage and is a foundation to build intimacy in the relationship. We must be intentional to protect quality time in our marriage or else life's issues will undermine the intimacy, bond and emotional connection in the marriage relationship.

Prayer:

Father, be a wall of defense around our marriage. Shield it from any outside force that would attempt to divide and destroy what you have established. Thank you for wisdom and insight regarding the things that are good for our marriage. Reveal, expose and remove anything that may be a barrier. Never let us be ignorant of satan's devices.

In Jesus' Name, Amen.

Day 8

Marriage is More than Sex

Marriage is more than sex. I can remember when the reality of marriage first hit Jessie and I. We were young newlyweds with raging hormones. In our world, the top activity on our priority list was sex, sex...and more sex! We eventually had a reality check and recognized that it was going to take more than sex to keep a marriage together.

Marriage takes work. It is a never ending *work in progress*. This is something we had to learn early in our marriage. One dictionary defines a, "*work in progress,*" as something that has entered the production process, but is not yet a finished product. The day that a couple has their first argument, the process has begun! It is during the process that some couples will either be refined by the fire or disgruntled and dissolved. This is the reality of marriage.

The world has painted this false image of marriage. It is idealized by a glamorous wedding, the perfect honeymoon, a beautiful home (*of course with children*), and a wonderful life together that has no challenges or obstacles to overcome. Most newlyweds get a reality check within the first two or three years of marriage. It seems that everything starts off great and then things take a turn and you soon find yourselves in a heated argument, expectations aren't met and you begin to wonder what have you gotten yourself into...The process has begun!

All couples disagree at times. If you divorce and remarry, you will still disagree with the new spouse. Why? Because you are two imperfect people with different views, opinions, backgrounds, values and expectations who are now joined together in covenant to build your lives together. There will be challenges to overcome, but the reward is so sweet if you can endure the process.

While in the process, take every experience and learn from it. Pray, meditate on God's word and seek Godly counsel if necessary to help you endure the process. When you receive Godly instructions, follow them. Stop focusing on your spouse and what they may or may not be doing. Ask God, "***What am I supposed to do?***" When He tells you, don't be surprised if it goes against what you want to do.

Remember, there is a bigger picture than what you may be able to see right now. Don't abandon the process. God is a God of restoration and He's able to make all things new. He that shall endure until the end, the same shall be saved (see Matthew 24:13).

Prayer:

Father, thank you for faith and strength to endure the process. Holy Spirit, lead us and guide us as we journey together. Help us to remain steadfast and not abandon the process of growth and maturity in our marriage relationship. In every experience, help us to come out wiser, stronger and better.

In Jesus' Name, Amen.

Day 9

Make Marriage Better

In marriage, we should thoughtfully consider ways to make our marriage better. No matter how long we've been married, there is always an opportunity for improvement. Each marriage is different and has its specific needs. We must examine what the needs are in our own marriage and make a concerted effort to make our marriage better. Here are a few suggestions that may be helpful:

- **Take time to communicate**. Be intentional to not only speak, but to also listen with the intent to resolve whatever issue is at hand
- **Be more affectionate towards your spouse**. Sometimes a simple touch can be more powerful than a word spoken.
- **Find ways to help your spouse** *(ie. with chores, children, errands, etc.)*
- **Block out quality time for you and your spouse**. There is nothing like taking out time to show your spouse that he or she is a priority. Block out time for just the two of you and refuse to allow others to snatch it!

- **Pray together**. Matthew 18:20 reads, "*Where two or three gather together in my name, there am I with them.*" If couples can simply learn to pray together, and invite God into their marriage and home, they will experience a oneness that can't be disturbed by any outside force.
- **Exercise together**. Promotes a healthy lifestyle, teamwork and allows you to support and encourage each other while on your journey to getting fit.
- **Set goals together and talk about a plan to achieve those goals**. Have you heard the saying, "*teamwork makes the dream work*?" So it is in marriage, when a couple comes to together, and set themselves to work as a team to achieve a common goal, there is nothing that can stop them!

Remember, every step to become a better spouse is one step closer to creating a better marriage. There is no goal too small when it comes to making marriage better.

The latter part of John 10:10 reads, "*I am come that they might have life, and that they might have it more abundantly.*" God wants us to experience His abundance in every area of our lives, including our marriage.

- If your marriage is okay, set a goal to make it good.
- If your marriage is good, set a goal to make it better.
- If your marriage is better, set a goal to make this the best year yet!

Prayer:

Father, just as you've presented Your best to us when you gave your son, Jesus Christ, to die for our sins, help us to always present our best to You in our marriage relationship. Make clear to us what areas we need to make better, and give us creative ways to implement actions that will be a blessing to our spouse and our marriage relationship as a whole.

In Jesus' Name, Amen.

Day 10

Break the Routine

A quote from the book, "*The Purpose and Power of Love & Marriage*" written by Myles Munroe, states: "*When a married couple becomes too familiar with each other, a lot of the adventurous spontaneity goes out of their marriage. Marriage should be stable and strong, so that both partners feel secure, but within that environment, there should be room for adventure.*"

These are great words of wisdom that any couple can implement into their relationship. In marriage we must be careful not to fall into the pit of complacency. When this happens, couples begin to take each other for granted and the excitement of being together becomes a memory of the past.

It's so easy to get caught up into our daily routine. Before you know it, weeks have passed and you find yourself wondering why things are so "cold" in the house. At some point, there must be an interruption of your schedule to reconnect with your spouse. In other words ... *break the routine!*

Here are a few ideas to consider:

- Show up for lunch at your spouse's job

- Plan an overnight stay or perhaps a weekend getaway
- Take a spontaneous drive to the nearest beach to see the sunset
- Have a nice romantic dinner in the middle of the week
- Plan a fun date night
- Cook breakfast and serve your spouse in bed
- Read a book together and share your thoughts
- Prepare a nice bubble bath with candles
- Surprise your spouse with the ultimate massage
- Leave a love note or words of encouragement inside their lunch box
- Write a message on a mirror for them to see first thing in the morning
- Leave a love note in their vehicle to see when they leave for work
- Create a runway of roses in your bedroom
- Send messages of love via text and email throughout the day

These are just a few fun ideas to keep your marriage vibrant, alive and adventurous! Never let your marriage become stale and boring. There is always something you can do to revitalize your marriage. Never take your spouse for granted. Never assume they know you love them. Remember, it only takes a few minutes to build monumental memories in marriage.

When was the last time you did something spontaneous in your marriage? We present this challenge to you to surprise your spouse and do something different within the next week.

Prayer:

Father, thank You that love flourishes in our marriage daily and thank You that we experience an overflow of happiness and joy. Where we've fallen into a dry place, show us how to redeem the excitement of being together. Help us to enjoy each other so that we can keep our marriage fresh and satisfied. Give us creative ideas so that we can participate in creating a marriage full of life and priceless memories.

In Jesus' Name, Amen.

Day 11

Counting the Cost to Build a Strong Marriage

Many couples enter into marriage without counting the cost. In Luke 14:28-30, Although Jesus was speaking specifically of counting the cost of following Him as a disciple, His words provide wise counsel for couples who are entering or have entered into a marriage relationship.

When Jessie and I built our first home. There was so much involved in the preparation and building of our home. I remember going to pick out the property and making the initial investment to acquire the land. Then we had to select all the materials, colors, patterns and designs. At times, it seemed a bit overwhelming, but we knew that in order for our home to be what we wanted it to be, we had to go thru the process of seeing that every small detail was given attention. As we carefully inspected our home during this process, we noticed certain things that had to be re-done by the builder. It took a lot of patience and effort to see the project thru but once it was completed, we were so excited to move into our first home. Once we closed on our home and were handed the keys, we laughed about how it was the most stressful time in our marriage. The process was bitter at times, but so sweet in the end!

The same attention we give to building a house, we must give to building a home. There are couples who live in million dollar houses that are not homes. There is no love, peace or joy present in the home.

Marriage takes deliberate action from both the husband and wife. In order for marriage to work, there must be participation on both parts. Just like building a home, we must go thru the process:

- First, get a design (an image of what you want your marriage to look like). The blueprint should originate from the word of God (*God's design*) See Ephesians 5:21-33. These Godly principles should be referred to often in building a strong marriage.
- Next, inspect the foundation (a personal relationship with Jesus Christ and a desire to please Him first is essential to building a strong marriage). See Romans 10:9-10
- Be sure to stay connected with the General Contractor (the contractor has experience and knowledge on how to coordinate a project and bring it together; this

symbolizes staying connected to God and allowing Him to be your guide in the marriage). James 4:8 reads, "Draw nigh to God, and he will draw night to you."

- Next, select quality materials (these are things that you and your spouse are both willing to put into your marriage; what you put into it - is what you will get out of it!) Quality materials can be found in Galatians 5:22-23 "But the fruit of the Spirit is love, joy, peace, longsuffering, gentleness, goodness, faith, meekness, temperance."
- Don't forget you need committed workers (you and your spouse must be willing to allow God to work in and thru you to build the marriage). Ephesians 3:20 reads, "Now unto him that is able to do exceeding abundantly above all that we are able to ask or think, according to the power that *worketh in us.*"

These are just a few steps that we are reminded of in the building process. Although every home is unique, these important nuggets can be applied to every marriage relationship and will ensure that you and your spouse walk through a threshold of love and faith knowing that God is working through your marriage to accomplish His purpose.

Prayer:

Father, help us to stay committed to working out the plans that You have for our marriage. We choose to build our marriage upon a solid foundation, which is the word of God. In our own ability, we can't build a strong marriage, but we can do all through thru Christ that strengthens us. We surrender to You. We are willing workers. Thank You for making our house a home.

In Jesus' Name, Amen.

Day 12

Becoming Best Friends

A husband and wife should know each other better than they know anyone else – *this includes knowing the good, bad and the ugly!*

In marriage, your spouse should be your best friend. Some people will share things with a best friend before family, and in some cases that friend may know more about you than a blood relative.

A best friend loves you for you - with all of your imperfections. They don't judge or criticize you, but speak the truth to you in love. They are your biggest fan and will encourage you and celebrate you all the way to the finish line.

Many marriages fail to reach this dimension of intimacy and friendship. There is no communication and openness and the marriage has yet to take off from surface level.

Every husband and wife should challenge themselves to take the realm of friendship to another level in their marriage. Spend time with your spouse. Make your spouse, your confidant. Share your dreams, goals and intimate thoughts. Take the time to really get to know each other as best friends.

Prayer:

Father, thank you for strengthening the bond of friendship in our marriage. Help us to develop a trust and closeness that is unique from any other relationship besides You. Help us to open ourselves to experience a new realm of friendship founded upon Your love. Remove any barriers that will prevent us from connecting and strengthening the bond of friendship in our marriage.

In Jesus 'Name, Amen.

Day 13

Turn Down the Volume

Have you heard the saying, "*It's not what you say, but how you say it?*"

It's unfortunate that there are many married couples who can only express their feelings or point of view by yelling and screaming at each other. What does this accomplish? Some truly believe that this type of communication is effective, but in actuality, it's an automatic barrier to resolving issues and a behaviour that leads to total shut-down. In addition, this type of interaction demonstrates a lack of maturity, discipline and respect.

Can a problem truly be resolved or the root of an issue addressed when couples are screaming and yelling at each other? Also, in addition to tone, what if facial expressions and attitudes are all out of whack? How does this type of behavior contribute to effective communication in the marriage relationship? Furthermore, if children are involved, what sort of message are you making loud and clear for them to see? In other words, what kind of example are you setting for your children regarding the proper way to resolve conflict?

In the book, ***Love and Respect***, by Dr. Emerson Eggerichs, it states that "**you can be right, but wrong at the top of your voice".** In marriage, you will have disagreements, but we must learn to express our point of view in a respectful and disciplined manner.

Sometimes it may mean that you need to step away to gather yourself and pray so that you can properly manage your emotions. Whatever the case may be, remember to **turn down the volume** because screaming and yelling only leads to a dead-end. Prov. 15:1 (KJV) reads, "*a soft answer turneth away wrath: but grievous words stir up anger.*"

Prayer:

Father, thank you for the Holy Spirit who is our helper. We rely on You to teach us how to effectively communicate with our spouse. Let us be quick to listen, slow to speak, and slow to anger. Let us always speak the truth in love. Our desire is to please You in our actions toward each other. Remove barriers, behaviors and attitudes that work against our oneness. We submit our will to Your will.

In Jesus Name, Amen.

Day 14

Recognize Who the Real Enemy Is

Don't get blindsided! It's time to recognize who the real enemy is in marriage.

If couples are not careful to recognize the enemy and his tactics to destroy marriage, they can easily find themselves caught up in the trap of discord, confusion and disagreement. John 10:10 (KJV) reads, "*The thief cometh not but for to steal, and to kill, and to destroy ...*" Ephesians 4:27 (KJV) reads "*... give no place to the devil.*"

Many fires can be extinguished sooner than later if couples would begin to recognize or discern who the real enemy is ... *it's not your spouse.*

Ephesians 6:12-13 (TLB) says, "*For we are not fighting against people made of flesh and blood, but against persons without bodies—the evil rulers of the unseen world, those mighty satanic beings and great evil princes of darkness who rule this world; and against huge numbers of wicked spirits in the spirit world.*" [13] *So use every piece of God's armor to resist the enemy whenever he attacks, and when it is all over, you will still be standing up.*

Prayer is the key to making us spiritually aware of the methods the devil uses to attempt to destroy our marriage. Prayer discerns division and is the communication line to download specific instructions on how to defeat any tactic or scheme the devil is attempting to conjure up in our marriage. My mom used to say, "The devil don't have no new tricks!" The sooner couples realize their spouse is not their enemy, they can begin to fight in the spirit realm to defeat the "real enemy".

Prayer:

Father, help us to be aware of the attacks sent to destroy our marriage. Let us not be ignorant of Satan's devices. Help us to always see beyond the surface of conflict to spiritually discern who the real enemy is. Stir up the warrior in us that would cause us to be on the offense rather than the defense as it relates to protecting our covenant. Keep us united on the battlefield as we keep each other covered in prayer. Let us not be passive in protecting what you have ordained, but let us always be persistent in Your will and our love towards You and each other.

In Jesus' Name, Amen.

Day 15

In It to Win It! Stay Committed

Jesus Christ was committed all the way to the cross. He was lied on, mocked, betrayed, taunted, whipped, beaten and crucified for us. While enduring the suffering, He could have said "Forget it", "I can't do this", "It's too difficult," but He was committed to endure because He knew of the resurrection to come and the promise of eternal life for both you and I.

Psalm 37:5 (KJV) reads, "*Commit thy way unto the Lord*". Just as Christ is committed to us, we should be committed to Him. If more couples would commit to Christ first, it would set the standard to commit to each other. Many couples have taken the easy way out and have failed to stay committed. When challenges come, as they will, they choose to bail out and say, "forget it." They fail to commit to the covenant, which affects their commitment to their spouse.

Do you think it was easy for Christ to endure what He did? Absolutely not, but He was committed. It's time for couples to commit to the covenant, put in the work and stay together until the "resurrection" day in their marriage. You may be facing a challenge right now in your marriage and wondering how will victory come out of this? Don't bail out - that's the easy way.

Commit to God, Commit to Pray, Commit to Listen, Commit to Obey, and then EXPECT a resurrection in your marriage!

Jessie and I made a decision to commit to three things early in our young married life. Those three things are: 1) Commit our lives to God 2) Commit to being faithful to each other 3) Commit to stay in the marriage and work it out no matter what issues come up and how difficult it seems.

Although we made these commitments, it doesn't mean they haven't been challenged. There is a big misconception that once you get married, you won't have any conflicts, challenges or issues to work out. After all the wedding bliss is over, couples soon realize that now they must find a way to make the marriage work.

Marriage is a wonderful thing, but it takes work! Issues in marriage can't be resolved unless ***both*** parties are committed to working it out. In order to work it out, we must do three things:

1) **Forgive:** Forgiveness is a decision and it is key to moving forward in any relationship. For some, forgiveness comes more easily than others. In any event, we must trust God and know that He has given us the ability to forgive. Philippians 4:13 reads, "*I can do all things through Christ who strengthens me.*" If you trust in your own ability, you may never forgive, but if you trust in God to give you the strength to forgive (in order that you can please Him), God will help you to forgive, just has He has forgiven you. Mark 11:25 says, "*And when ye stand praying, forgive, if*

ye have ought against any; that your Father also which is in heaven may forgive you your trespasses."

2) **Change:** Resolving issues in marriage include ***both*** the husband and wife making a decision to do something different. Many couples can't move forward because they refuse to embrace change in the relationship. True repentance involves turning away from the old and embracing the new. This requires a heart and mind change. Unless this happens, in many cases, the conduct or behavior remains the same. Both spouses should take the focus off of each other and ask themselves this question, *"What changes do I need to personally make to move this relationship from being stuck to pressing forward and being strong?"* Then, commit to change and be obedient to the instructions that God gives you. Trust God to help you to make the necessary adjustments whether in attitude, communication or deed. Keep your eyes on God and expect to see improvement in the relationship.

3**) Let Go of The Past**: In addition to ***forgiveness*** and ***change***, there must be a willingness to ***let the past go and move forward***. Every day is a new opportunity to move forward, but many couples can't move forward because they won't let the past go. Philippians 3:12-14 (MSG) reads, *"I'm not saying that I have this all together, that I have it made. But I am well on my way, reaching out for Christ, who has so wondrously reached out for me. Friends, don't get me wrong: By no means do I count myself an expert* *in all of this, but I've got my eye on the goal, where God is beckoning us onward—to Jesus. I'm off and running, and I'm not turning back."* Couples must learn to let it go and not turn back!

Quote: "Coming together is the beginning. Keeping together is progress. Working together is success" ~ Henry Ford

Prayer:

Father, just as you were committed all the way to the cross, we in turn commit our lives and our marriage to You. Even in difficulty, we choose to trust You and remain committed to the covenant. Holy Spirit, have Your way in our lives. Strengthen us and renew the desire to stay committed. Thank you for being a faithful God and for resurrecting every dead area in our marriage. Holy Spirit, help us to forgive, help us to change, help us to let go of the past and help us to keep moving forward!

In Jesus' Name, Amen.

Day 16

Keep Marriage "*Sexy*"

For some, this may seem like a superficial topic to talk about, but the truth of the matter is, many couples struggle in their marriage and are no longer attracted to each other because the marriage lacks "*sexiness*".

The intention here is not to be "deep" but very practical. Some spouses think that once you get married, physical attraction is no longer important. They no longer put the same effort into sprucing themselves up for their spouse as they did when they first met. Did I say for your spouse? Absolutely! True enough, real beauty stems from within and our spouse should truly love us for who we are on the inside, but let's not forget that our spouses have eyes too.

How many husbands and wives do you know that have, "Let themselves go?"

I remember my marriage mentor telling me long ago, that just because your husband is a man of God who loves God and has chosen to remain faithful to you, doesn't mean you should take him for granted. I've taken this wisdom to heart. Never take your spouse for granted. Have you heard the old saying, *"Whatever it took to get them, it takes to keep them?"*

I totally remember when I first laid eyes upon Jessie, I was taken away at how ***GOOD*** he looked to me! Whew!! We've shared with couples on many occasions the story about how we met and how physical attraction was very much a part of why I was into him and he was into me. I'm just being honest.

Once we were married and time passed, we obviously began to learn about the woes and joys of marriage and we grew to love each other beyond physical attraction. With 31 years of marriage, we've certainly had to mature and realize our physical appearance is a bit different from when we first met. We've both changed. We may not have the physique of a bodybuilder, or "brick-house" measurements, (some of you know about that), but we've both chosen to make the best of what we do have so that we can glorify God in our bodies, we can feel good about ourselves and we can keep the physical attraction in our marriage.

What was the first thing that caught your attention about your spouse? Internal qualities are obviously a priority, but let's keep it real. Was it his or her personality, conversation, talent, intellect, demeanor or overall physical attractiveness that first caught your attention? Some might say that it was a combination of things. Furthermore, when was the last time you looked upon your spouse and was attracted to him or her in a physical way?

I've heard the saying, *"Beauty is in the eye of the beholder."* What an accurate statement. No one can truly define what your spouse considers to be beautiful when they look upon you. Only you know what it took to captivate the heart of your spouse and cause them to want to be with you for the rest of his or her life.

There are couples today who consider this topic to be superficial and important only in the beginning of their relationship. Some feel that once they get married, physical attraction should take a back seat to deeper needs. I would suggest that keeping yourself up and remaining physically attractive to your spouse is important and should not be ignored in marriage.

Keeping the physical attraction in your marriage not only enhances the relationship, but helps to keep it stimulated and strong - yet taking away another tool that the devil uses to destroy marriages.

Prayer:

Father, thank you for the love, connection and attraction that exists between me and my spouse. Let us never take each other for granted. Help us to be excellent in everything that we do so that we may honor You in our marriage. We acknowledge and recognize that our body does not belong to us according to 1 Corinthians 6:19. We declare that we are disciplined and make wise choices as it relates to our spiritual and physical well-being. We want to be fit from the inside out. Reveal to us those things we need to do to keep our marriage healthy, sexy, and our desire for each other stimulated.

In Jesus' Name, Amen.

Day 17

Unity! ... Not Just About Me

The lack of oneness causes many couples to experience problems in their marriage. If you had a traditional wedding, do you remember lighting the unity candle during your wedding ceremony? The unity candle was symbolic of the man and woman leaving behind their two separate lives to become a new creation of oneness in covenant with God. Ask yourself this question, *"Is our flame of oneness still burning brightly today?"*

Mark 10:8-9 (AMP) reads, "*And the two shall become one flesh, so that they are no longer two, but one flesh. What therefore God has united (joined together), let not man separate or divide.*" Problems arise in marriage when either the husband or wife decides to devote to their *own* flame rather than ignite the flame they share with their spouse. He or she begins to place their own selfish desires ahead of their spouse and it becomes *"all about me"*.

In order to have a healthy marriage, you can't have a selfish mindset. It can no longer be "I", but "Us." Couples should not underestimate the power of unity and agreement in a marriage relationship. Husband and wives who purpose to protect this area in their marriage, and refuse to allow division to set in, will experience success, peace and advancement in their relationship. Beware of the things that will keep you divided in your marriage like unforgiveness, lack of communication, hardness of heart, disagreement, selfishness and violation of trust. These characteristics lead to destruction. We should be careful to cultivate and protect unity in our marriage. Here is an **I.D.E.A.** to promote unity in your marriage:

- **I**dentify areas of disunity and make every effort to resolve differences in a loving way.
- **D**on't lead private lives. Be open with each other. Choose sacredness over secrecy.
- **E**ngage in activities together (i.e. worship, prayer, extra-curricular activities, intimacy, etc.); Promote oneness
- **A**ct on a solution when challenges arise; Let the word of God be your guide. Share and communicate.

Prayer:

Father, we humble ourselves before You. Help us to live in a spirit of unity and oneness. We welcome peace into our hearts and into our home. Remove those thoughts and acts that would cause discord and disunity. Bind us together as one and help us to always remember that we can do more together than apart.

In Jesus' Name, Amen.

Day 18

Building Up Marriage in Our Community

A while ago, I called a radio station when the question was asked, "*What can we do as a community to help marriages*?"

My response was, "Those of us who are married should be a positive example or role model of a Godly marriage in our home, church, businesses and community. We should take the time to give back and help those who are on this journey of marriage. If we have had any measure of success, this is a starting point of encouraging another couple along the way."

In this day and time, you hear so much negativity about marriage, infidelity and divorce. It's refreshing and encouraging when you encounter a married couple who is genuinely happy to be married and enjoying life with their spouse. It doesn't mean that they don't have challenges, but they've made a decision to stand firm in their covenant relationship and are committed to God and to each other to work thru the bumps and bruises knowing that on the other side of every test, there are two people who are stronger, wiser and have embraced a deeper love for one another. Most importantly, you and your spouse are ***making a positive statement that marriage works*** - and what a difference Christ can make in your marriage.

Also, we should use every opportunity that we can to speak positively about the covenant of marriage. Whenever I hear of longevity in marriage, I congratulate and celebrate that couple. No matter where you are, at some point, you are bound to run into someone who may inadvertently begin to share about the challenges they are facing, particularly in the area of marriage. This is our opportunity to be an encouragement and support. You may not have all the answers, know all the right scriptures or have a huge catalog of marital advice, but you can give a testimony of what God has done for you in your marriage. You would be surprised at how this could be the very thing that encourages a man or woman to stay in their relationship and work it out.

Never underestimate the things that God has done your marriage. Testimonies are powerful. People are seeking realness and truth about how to have a successful marriage. They need witnesses of winning marriages. When we share our marital testimony, it then becomes an encouragement for others to believe God for their marriage. Mark 5:19 (NASB) reads, "*Go home to your people and report to them what great things the Lord has done for you, and how He had mercy on you." God is no respector of person*, Acts 10:34. Just as God continues to bless others in covenant, He can do the same for your marriage.

Prayer:

Father, thank you that wherever we go we can be a beacon of light in our community sharing with others the beauty of the marriage covenant. Lord, continue to perfect everything that concerns us so that we may be an effective witness and powerful presence in our community. We choose to follow the word of God as our guide so that we can have a productive and fruitful marriage. As couples cross our path and opportunities are created to talk about marriage, let our conversation always be one to edify and build up the covenant that You have created.

In Jesus' Name, Amen.

Day 19

Appreciating Acts of Kindness

Acts of kindness in a marriage should be noticed and appreciated.

I was blessed to attend an awesome women's conference years ago. The theme was "Divinely Favored". I will never forget this experience because the teaching was so awesome and reminded us of the favor of God that has been graciously given to us as sons and daughters of the King. Favor is defined as something done or granted out of good will, excessive kindness or preferential treatment.

Among many things shared, we were reminded that God's favor grants us supernatural advantages and it influences the heart of others to act on our behalf. Also, as people show favor towards us, we should be willing to show favor towards others. One way that we can show favor to others is by blessing them with acts of kindness.

When was the last time you blessed your spouse with an act of kindness? When was the last time you told your spouse, "*Thank You*"? Acts of kindness in a marriage should be noticed and appreciated. We should never get to the point where we take the kindness of our spouse for granted.

Take a moment to think about something your spouse has done for you recently and share with them a kind word or note to let them know that you've noticed their efforts, sacrifice or care. Galatians 5:22-23 (TLB) reads, "*But when the Holy Spirit controls our lives he will produce this kind of fruit in us: love, joy, peace, patience,* ***kindness,*** *goodness, faithfulness, gentleness and self-control.*"

Prayer:

Father, thank you that my life is filled with the favor of God and I receive excessive kindness everywhere I go. Help me to always recognize when favor and kindness is extended towards me. Teach me to be swift and obedient in extending that same favor and kindness to others, especially to my spouse.

In Jesus' Name, Amen

Day 20

Don't Say It!

How many times have you been in a conversation with your spouse and thought to yourself, ***"Don't say it!"*** You had formed the words in your mind and were prepared to let them flip from your lips – but then you caught yourself!

Can we be real? This usually happens when your spouse has "rubbed you the wrong way." In situations like this, it is important to practice temperance. What is temperance? Temperance is self-restraint in action; self-control. In Galatians 5:23, we find that temperance is also a fruit of the Spirit or an attribute of a Christian life.

Remember, once words are spoken, they are in the atmosphere and can't be taken back. Many couples spend years trying to recover from painful words spoken during the heat of an argument.

Conflict in marriage needs to be resolved in a productive way. Both spouses should be able to communicate their thoughts and concerns without using words that will belittle, alienate, intimidate or show disrespect. If neither spouse is able to do that, there needs to be time for you to step away, gather yourself and come back to the conversation at a more appropriate time - with a more appropriate tone. In some cases, couples may need a mediator. Whatever the case may be, it is wise to refrain from using words that will ultimately cause further pain in your relationship. In other words, it is better to hold your tongue than to say something you'll regret! James 1:19 reads, "*Understand this: everyone must be quick to hear, slow to speak, and slow to anger.*"

Ephesians 4:29 reads, "*Let no corrupt communication proceed out of your mouth, but that which is good to the use of edifying, that it may minister grace unto the hearers.*"

Prayer:

Father, we invite you into our communication with our spouse. Give us wisdom and help us to think before we speak. We submit ourselves to You. Lord, we want to exemplify the attributes of Your spirit, even in the most difficult times of communicating. Let love, patience, understanding and temperance reign in our communication with our spouse. Help us to be disciplined and led by Your spirit, so that we can resolve disagreements in a healthy and productive way that pleases You.

In Jesus' Name, Amen.

Day 21

Covenant Keepers

Many couples enter into marriage without considering the sacredness of covenant. They are more focused on the wedding performance than the solemn promise being made. I must admit that when we got married, we knew marriage was sacred, but didn't understand the depth of covenant. A marriage covenant is defined as a solemn (sacred, devotional, serious) and binding promise meant to last a lifetime.

God is very serious about covenant. In Psalm 89:3 (NLT) reads, *"No, I will not break my covenant; I will not take back a single word I said."* God is so serious about covenant that He sacrificed His only Son to give us a promise (covenant) of eternal life (see John 3:16).

Deuteronomy 7:9 reads, *"Know therefore that the Lord your God is God; He is the faithful God, keeping His covenant of love to a thousand generations of those who love Him and keep his commandments."* This scripture lets us know that God is a covenant keeping God - faithful to honor covenant.

Just as God honors covenant, we should honor covenant in our marriage. Just as God is faithful, we should be faithful in our marriage. Just as God is a covenant keeper, we should be covenant keepers in our marriage.

As married couples, we should never take our commitment to the covenant lightly. Our honor and commitment to this promise will be reflected in our actions towards our spouse.

Prayer:

Father, thank you for being a covenant keeping God. Just as you've demonstrated your faithfulness in our lives, let us demonstrate our love and faithfulness to You and each other. Let us never take the covenant of marriage lightly but let us always honor the covenant, hold it in high regard and respect the sacredness of the gift You have given to us in marriage.

In Jesus' Name, Amen.

Day 22

Kick Selfishness Out!

Jesus demonstrated His love unselfishly when He gave His life for our sins. To be imitators of Christ, we must learn to kick selfishness out of our marriage.

Selfishness does not have a place in marriage. It is demonstrated when a spouse has no regard to the feelings or concerns of their mate. It's no longer what can I do to please my spouse, but rather how can I get my own needs, wants and desires met. Having this attitude is a sure way to cause division and even resentment in a marriage.

God created marriage for both husband and wife to enjoy. The wife's desire should be to please her husband; and the husband's desire should be to please his wife. This requires an unselfish heart and willingness to love beyond yourself. Philippians 2:3-5 (NIV) states, *"Do nothing out of selfish ambition or vain conceit. Rather, in humility value others above yourselves, not looking to your own interests but each of you to the interests of the others. In your relationship with one another, have the same mindset as Christ Jesus."*

Wow! This scripture speaks volumes! Take a moment to think about the state of your marriage. Do you see areas of unspoken selfishness? Are you and your spouse collectively considering each other's needs and wants or are the benefits to your marriage one-sided?

Prayer:

Father, thank you for demonstrating the ultimate sacrifice of unselfish love towards us by giving your son Jesus Christ to die for our sins. Search our hearts God. Remove any stench of selfishness and replace it with the same self-sacrificing love you've demonstrated to us over and over again. We repent for those times that we took our spouse for granted and failed to consider his/her needs. As we follow you, thank you that we are free from selfishness, considerate of our spouse and daily living by the spirit of God.

In Jesus' Name, Amen.

Day 23

Marriage Needs "Time"

Marriage needs ***TIME***. Les Parrott writes in his book, ***Your Time-Starved Marriage***, *"The first step in reclaiming your time as a couple is to realize that your life is happening now. Not someday. Not once something else is achieved or a certain phase has passed. It's happening today. This is it. Now."*

I can remember when our son and daughter were still in elementary, middle and high school. It seemed as if our days flew by. Life was nonstop from pick-up and drop-offs to school, dance, football, cheerleading, meetings, work and ministry. Days and sometimes weeks would go by before Jessie and I had quality time together. It was never intentional to deprive our marriage of time, but it happened. Then, it was as if one day we had a wake-up call. We realized our marriage couldn't survive on rotating doors. We had to purpose to make time for our marriage. Not only was the time necessary and good to strengthen our marriage, but it also allowed our kids to see daddy and mommy loving each other and having time together.

The time that marriage needs doesn't require money. It could be a cuddle on the sofa, a stroll in the park or maybe a ride in the car for ice cream (we've done this on many occasions). The point is to slow down and reconnect with your spouse.

When First Lady Michelle Obama was interviewed and asked about the solid relationship between her and President Barack Obama she stated in a video, "*Couples should have date nights because it's important for kids to know their parents are connecting. It also gives children a sense of security when they see their parents loving each other and spending time together.*"

These are great words of wisdom to preserve your marriage. Proverbs 4:13 reads, *"Take hold of instruction; do not let go. Guard her, for she is your life."*

Prayer:

Father, let us never forget that marriage needs quality time. Help us to be sensitive to the temperature of our marriage. Even in our hectic schedules, remind us to carve out time to reconnect with our spouse and rekindle the romance. Let us never neglect each other, nor take each other for granted. Beginning today, we commit to giving our marriage the time that it needs.

In Jesus' Name, Amen.

Day 24

A Quality Marriage

What actions are you taking to improve the quality of your marriage?

As mentioned earlier, this year we celebrated thirty-one years of marriage. We thank God for His faithfulness in our marriage and for many more blessed years to come! As we began to reflect on our growth as husband and wife, one thing that clearly stands out to us, and has allowed us to remain joyfully married (not tolerating each other) these past several years, is our follow-thru on taking action in the areas that we want to see our marriage strengthened.

Even though God honors the marriage covenant, it still requires action on our part to make our marriage work. We've learned that we must invest into our marriage if we want to receive a good return.

The circumstances in which we got married were not favorable for a young couple. We knew that we needed help. We've been intentional to invest in our marriage by going to marriage workshops and seminars every year. We've made these activities a priority and we put what we learn into action. We've also surrounded ourselves with other married couples who have the same desire to strengthen and grow their marriage. We've had positive influences in our lives who were faithful to God and to their spouses. Although we've made all of these intentional investments, we still had a lot of, "life lessons," to learn. Some lessons were very tough, but when the tests came, as they will, we've learned to work through our challenges and pass the test!

Jessie always says that I never want our marriage to be, "average." We've learned that the quality of our marriage will be the direct result of the time and effort we put into making it work. Many folks complain about their marriage, but are not willing to make the necessary adjustments and/or changes to make it better. James 2:20 (KJV) reads, *"faith without works is dead."*

What does the quality of your marriage look like? Is the fuel running low in your marriage tank? Is your marriage thriving or surviving?

Marriage maintenance is important. Just like a car needs regular maintenance – so it is in a marriage relationship. What is your next plan of action to enrich the quality of your marriage?

Prayer:

Father, we decree and declare that our marriage is thriving! Help us to be intentional to invest in our marriage so that we may continue to grow and be all that you have purposed for us to be. Thank you for surrounding us with Godly influences to encourage and help us along the way. We refuse to be an average couple. Let our marriage flourish and be a beacon of light to encourage others along the journey. Thank you for perfecting everything that concerns us. We trust you to be God in our marriage.

In Jesus' Name, Amen!

Day 25

Goal-Setting With Your Spouse

What is the point of being married if you have two people occupying the same house, each with their own agenda, doing their own thing and occasionally crossing paths along the way? How can dreams be achieved together? How can household goals be met? How can the family move forward?

When families come together and cooperate as a team, they will begin to see purposeful progression. Throughout the year, we should periodically assess our goals to see what we've accomplished and where we want to go (*personally, spiritually, professionally and collectively as a husband/wife/family*).

Jessie and I make it a practice to come together at the end of the year to review where we are and evaluate our goals for the future. We are focused to communicate with each other and confirm agreement as it relates to specific goals that concern our lives together.

Goals in marriage can't be achieved without agreement. Amos 3:3 (KJV) reads, *"Can two walk together, except they be agreed*?" Setting goals as husband and wife help to strengthen the relationship, cultivate communication, promote unity and teamwork in the household.

Below is a format that Jessie and I have personally used for goal setting. You and your spouse may want to consider using this format to guide your goal-setting discussion. Before you get started, it's important to schedule uninterrupted time so that you can both give your undivided attention. Also, it is important to have a pen and paper for taking notes. Habakkuk 2:2 reads, *"And the LORD answered me, and said, Write the vision, and make it plain upon tables, that he may run that readeth it."*

Budget Review

- Look at where you are financially and determine if any adjustments need to be made with the handling of finances.
- Discuss a plan for saving, sowing, investing, etc.
- Discuss new expenses that may be incurred or the next major household expense and what needs to be done to prepare for it
- Review debt and discuss payoffs (use a basic budget worksheet if necessary)
- Make sure your goals are attainable - don't try to do everything at once.

Discuss Household Goals

- Discuss home projects that need to be completed (*in and outside of the home*) so that you are both aware of them and in agreement of what needs to be done.

Discuss Goals as Husband & Wife

- What are some things you plan to do together? This may involve health and fitness, volunteer work, ministry, a business venture, relational goals, etc. Pursuing goals together promote oneness in the relationship.

Discuss Personal Goals

- What are personal goals that each of you have as it relates to education, career, ministry, health and fitness, hobbies, etc. It's important to have goals together, but it's also important to have personal goals. Each spouse should talk about their personal goals so that the other spouse may know how to encourage, support and pray for the other. One thing that Jessie and I do is create vision boards so that each of us have a visual reminder of what the other's goals are and encourage each other in our action plans.

Discuss Future Vacations and Family Outings

- Discuss vacation plans. When and where do you want to go? Do research on the destination and determine lodging, airfare and a detailed budget.

Discuss/Schedule Fun Dates

- Discuss activities you can do together without the kids. When and where do you want to go? Do you want to invite friends? Perhaps a weekend get-away, weekly dates, etc.

Coordinate Your Calendars

- Decide if you are in synch with your calendars. Work towards an agreement on commitments, especially if they affect your quality time planned.

Review Your Progress

- Choose a time to review the status of your goals and determine if you need to change anything.

Communicate! Communicate! Communicate!

- Never stop talking! Keep the lines of communication open.
- Discuss if there are any open topics to be revisited? Take time to discuss them thoroughly.
- Share progress along the journey.

Prayer

- Implement daily prayer time so that you can pray specifically about your family goals. When a husband and wife prays together, it promotes intimacy and unity in the marriage.

Psalm 20:4 – (NIV) May He give you the desire of your heart and make all of your plans succeed.

Prayer:

Father, thank You for our time to come together to focus on Your faithfulness. We thank you for what You've done and the things that You are going to do. As we begin to assess our goals, look at where we are and where we want to go, we seek You for guidance, wisdom and insight. Holy Spirit, order our steps in all of our goal-setting. You said in Matthew 18:20 where two or three gather in Your name, there you are among them. So we invite You in to help us to work together as a team so that we can move forward accomplishing all that God has purposed for us in this coming year. We know that there is nothing too hard for You. Thank you that your favor surrounds us in all of our endeavors. This is our year for complete and total victory!

In Jesus' Name, Amen.

Day 26

Help Us To Communicate!

Communication is a key component necessary to have a successful marriage. The absence of communication in marriage leads to chaos! Discussing this topic can never get old because as long as two people remain in relationship, there will always be a need to communicate. Healthy marriages are built on good communication. No matter how long a couple has been married, I would venture to say that there is always an opportunity to improve in the area of communication.

In marriage, there are many contributing factors that influence how we communicate. It could be our upbringing, environment, customs, experiences, parenting, as well as beliefs – *just to name a few*. It is important that couples set the tone for how they will communicate early in the relationship (even before marriage). Determine what is acceptable and unacceptable behavior when communicating.

Although this is a topic that could take months to dissect, here are just a few nuggets to ***H.E.L.P.*** when communicating in marriage:

H ave a designated time to connect; Timing is important. Make sure there are no distractions. Be open and honest with your spouse about how you feel. Know what to say and how to say it.

Don't be critical or judgmental, but speak the truth in love. (See Ephesians 4:15)

E ffective communication is key. Keep emotions under control. If emotions are too intense and the conversation is heated, communication *will not* be effective. Step back and revisit the topic at another time.

L ook for resolution – not retaliation. Listen closely to what is being said before responding. Above all pursue peace.

P ray in advance that God will prepare your spouse's heart to receive what you have to share. Invite God into the conversation and pray that you receive wisdom in sharing with your spouse.

Remember poor communication hinders progress in marriage! Don't get stuck in the zone of silence!

Prayer:

Holy Spirit, we call upon you our Helper and we ask that you would help us in the area of communication. Lead and guide us as we express what is in our heart. We know the devil comes to steal, kill and to destroy marriages, but we choose to win in the area of communication. Give us effective ways to share with each other and help us to respond in love and with grace - even with the most difficult topics. Father, help us to seek resolution with every discussion so that we can move forward. We surrender our thoughts to you. We surrender our will to you. We surrender our mouth to you. We surrender our heart to you.

In Jesus' Name, Amen.

Day 27

7 Keys to Empower Your Marriage

We have learned many lessons within our thirty-one years of marriage, however, we firmly believe that these seven principles have held firm as a monumental guide to building a successful marriage:

1. **Fortify the Foundation**: Make God the foundation of your marriage and honor the marriage covenant. It must begin with a personal relationship with God. Keep God First. Psalm 127:1 reads, *"Unless the Lord builds the house, they labor in vain that built it."*

2. **Invest Into Your Marriage**: It's important to invest into your marriage and spend quality time together. No matter how long you have been married, you can always make improvements. Marriage maintenance should be a priority. Luke 12:34 reads, *"For where your treasure is, there will your heart be also."* People will invest into what is important to them. The biggest investment is time.

3. **Communicate:** When communication stops, the marriage will die. Stay open to communication, which is both speaking

and listening. Be respectful. James 1:19 reads, *"Wherefore, my beloved brethren, let every man must be swift to hear, slow to speak, slow to wrath."*

4. **Forgive:** Forgiveness is a decision. You must master this area in marriage. Matthew 6:14-16 reads, *"For if you forgive others of their transgressions, your heavenly Father will also forgive you. But if you do not forgive others, neither will your Father forgive your trespasses."*

5. **Prayer**: Prayer is important in marriage. Implement prayer and learn to pray together. There is nothing more powerful than a husband and wife unified in prayer. Matthew 18:19 reads, *"Again I say unto you, that if two of you shall agree on earth as touching any thing that they shall ask, it shall be done for them of my Father which is in heaven."*

6. **Stay Unified**: No more "I", but "Us". Don't let anything or anybody create division in your marriage. Stay together. Ephesians 5:31 reads, *"... And they two shall be one flesh."*

7. **Protect Trust**: Once trust is violated, it can be a long road to recovery. Protect this area in your marriage. Proverbs 28:13 reads, "*He that covereth his sins shall not*

prosper: but whoso confesseth and forsaketh them shall have mercy."

Prayer:

Father, thank you for blessing our covenant. As we move forward in our marriage, help us to embrace Godly principles that will correct, restore and strengthen our marriage. We want to bring glory to You in all that we do.

In Jesus' Name, Amen.

Day 28

Keep Children in Their Place – *Not In Your Space*!

Over the years our family has grown. Not only are we parents, we are now grandparents. One of the greatest joys that a husband and wife can experience is the birth of a child. The Bible reads in Psalm 127:3 (KJV), *"Lo, children are an heritage of the Lord; and the fruit of the womb is his reward."*

As parents we should love and nurture our children, but also teach them to respect the parameters of our marriage. Many couples put the primary focus of the family on the children and neglect to nurture the marriage relationship. As a result, marriage becomes secondary to the demands of the children. In some cases, children completely dominate the home and their influence dictates the parent's schedule, communication, as well as quality time together. This type of ongoing interference can be stressful in a marriage relationship.

We must keep in mind that although the dynamics of each family may be different, the principle of order remains the same ... *Children should be kept in their place – not in your space*!

Children should experience and see our example of love while being taught to respect authority in the home, as well as the sacredness of our marriage. As parents, it's our responsibility to establish order based on the word of God.

Ephesians 5:23-25 (KJV) reads, *"For the husband is the head of the wife, even as Christ is the head of the church: and he is the Savior of the body. Therefore as the church is subject unto Christ, so let the wives be to their own husbands in everything. Husbands, love your wives, even as Christ also loved the church, and gave himself for it."*

By following the scripture, the husband is to be a loving leader in the home and provide oversight of all matters of the home. The husband sets the tone for the home with his willingness to serve as the leader, loving his wife as Christ loves the church, sacrificing for his family, providing protection, provision and guidance for the family. He in fact should love his wife in the same manner he loves his own body (see Ephesians 5:28).

Genesis 2:18 makes clear that God created the wife to be the husband's helper. God knew that man would need assistance to steward his responsibilities. Wives are to serve and support by helping to bring the vision of the family unit to fruition. Also, according to Ephesians 5:22, the wife is to submit to her husband as unto the Lord. Many women do not like to hear the “s-word”. They fail to see that when they submit to their husband, and put themselves under his leadership, they are actually submitting to God. Submission should be a wife’s response because of her love and reverence towards God. Submission is not mindless obedience and doesn’t devalue the wife, but it is God’s ordained structure for the marriage.

In a balanced marriage, couples should consult each other about family decisions, however, in the event a decision can’t be agreed upon, the husband (as leader of the home), makes the final decision knowing that he is ultimately responsible to God.

Ephesians 6:1-2 establishes that children should obey their parents in the Lord, for this is right. They are to honor their father and mother, which is the first commandment with promise.

The world today has gotten away from God’s original structure for the family. As believers we have a responsibility to establish order in our homes.

When there is no order, structure or discipline enforced, it can cause many problems and may even lead to divorce!

Prayer:

Father, we thank you for entrusting us with our children. We know that they are a blessing from you. We declare that our children are taught of the Lord and obedient to Your will. Great is their peace and undisturbed composure. Thank you Father that our children grow in wisdom and stature, and in favor with God and men. We declare that our children are not conformed to the ways of this world. We seek You for wisdom and guidance in how to be properly parent our children without neglecting the sacredness of our marriage. Help us to establish order in our home according to the word of God, so that love, joy and peace may abide.

In Jesus' Name, Amen.

Day 29

Forgiveness

One of the greatest tactics the devil uses to destroy marriages is in the area of unforgiveness. At some point or another, we all will have to walk down the pathway of forgiveness. We will either be on the giving end or the receiving end.

Living a life of unforgiveness can wear you down spiritually, emotionally and physically. In your own ability, forgiving your spouse may seem impossible, but we must know that this is something that God expects and requires from us as His sons and daughters. The good news is that God will never ask us to do anything that is impossible for us to do!

You must remember that forgiveness is not just for your spouse, it's for you. If you are holding on to anger, bitterness and unforgiveness, it's difficult to walk in love. However, when you make a decision to forgive, you are then able to follow God's command and example to love one another as He loves us. John 13: 35 reads, *"by this shall all men know that ye are my disciples, if ye have love one to another."* Forgiveness is necessary to be a follower of Christ and it also allows us to demonstrate the same grace that has been given unto us. Matthew 6:14-15 reads, *"For if you forgive men their trespasses, your heavenly Father will also forgive you; But if ye forgive not men their trespresses, neither will your Father forgive your trespasses."*

We must know that God is our helper. If we rely on own strength, painful thoughts will prevent us from embracing the Godly attribute of forgiveness; but never underestimate the power of God! The Holy Spirit, living on the inside of you, will help you to forgive – even in the most difficult situations. Philippians 4:13 reads, *"I can do all things through Christ which strengtheneth me."* This is an encouraging scripture that reminds us that Christ lives on the inside of us and by His power, we can do ALL things!! Praise God!

Prayer:

Holy Spirit thank You for being my helper. My desire is to please You in every area of my life. I repent of my sins and ask that You forgive me. I release bitterness, anger and unforgiveness and I receive Your love, peace and joy. I choose to live free from offense. Mend every broken area in our marriage and heal our hearts. I choose to be led by Your spirit and not of my flesh. Help me to walk in a spirit of love and forgiveness, just as You love and forgive me. We know there is nothing too hard for you. We commit our marriage into your hands and surrender our will to Your will.

In Jesus' Name, Amen.

Day 30

Commit! Connect! Communicate!

In marriage, we never stop learning about each other. You would think that when a couple has had several weeks of premarital counseling, they have learned everything there is to know about the other, but that's simply not the case. Just when you think you know everything about your spouse - you learn something new.

We are continually evolving and for this reason we suggest you implement the 3 C's into your marriage:

- **Commit** – Commit to keep your marriage enriched. Never stop investing into your marriage.

- **Connect** – Don't get so busy that you fail to connect. Initiate times of intimacy and closeness by sharing your feelings, thoughts and desires. Be affectionate, touch and embrace each other. Keep loving gestures alive in the marriage. Pray for your spouse and pray together.

- **Communicate** – This topic has been mentioned several times throughout this book and can't be stressed enough. Keep lines of communication open. Be intentional to resolve issues. Seek wise counsel when necessary to help overcome challenges with communicating.

Prayer:

Father, thank you for a marriage that is full of life and ever growing. We commit to do those things that are necessary to keep us connected in our marriage. Our desire is to experience God's best in our marriage covenant and we commit to put in the work to keep our marriage enriched and connected.

In Jesus' Name, Amen

Stay Connected!

Email: heavenonearthmarriage@gmail.com

Website:
www.heavenonearthmarriageministry.com
www.kendrayadams.com

Made in the USA
Coppell, TX
02 February 2021

49362096R00059